The 'OLOGY' of G.A.M.E

Volume 1: The Introduction and Introspection of Game

Robert Web

Fulton Books
Meadville, PA

Published by Fulton Books 2023

ISBN 979-8-88731-772-4 (paperback)
ISBN 979-8-88731-773-1 (digital)

Printed in the United States of America

This book is dedicated to *game* or the grammatical avenue manipulating everything. My beautiful wife and children, family, good friends, and all those affiliated with game across the world. All the great, loving, and precious souls lost along the way. And special thanks to all the sources reviewed for these writings, including the wonderful and terrible characters that the writers had interactions with throughout their lives to produce such an encompassing and dynamic viewpoint.

Contents

Acknowledgments

God and the Holy Bible, my beautiful wife and children, the recognition of game, MSU of Denver, the rap gods E-40 and the late and great Pimp C, the late and great Ronoku Rashidi, the ingenious comedian Dave Chappelle, George Lucas for Star Wars, *a truly inspiring legacy. All sources listed in the bibliography. And all the great, loving, and cherished souls lost along the way!*

First and foremost, thank you for your purchase. That small purchase has equipped you with a powerful tool, *game*, and a semicomprehensive understanding of this concept and principle. Game is a true belief system in many circles that has produced uncanny results for those who utilize it efficiently. For over two decades of the writers' lives, the ology of game was truly their religion. And for over two decades of the writers' lives, the wonderful and dreadful character types that the writers had interactions with throughout have produced such an encompassing and dynamic viewpoint. So much so that as the reader interprets the writings, some statements may seem to be declarative; nevertheless, the writings contained within these volumes are not instructional. They are better understood as perspectival, influential observations. They leave the reader to glean the content contained within the volumes of the writings as the reader desires.

Clarity or specifically the ology of game, until this point, has been, to say the least, vague and ambiguous. This writing clarifies the principle of game. In addition, it also puts the ology behind it. The introduction of truly unique character concepts, defense and countermechanisms, thought processes, and definitive points of great wisdom are just pages away. The contents contained within these volumes are so dynamic that the writers will hopefully inspire a new subgenre entitled nonfiction (perspectival, influential observations). And on that, please believe that the writers' lives are more enriched with the benefit of game.

For those with busy lives, we completely understand, and that is why this writing and the series contained within the volumes are designed as rather quick reads that are comprehensive and to the point. This series will truly profit individual readers with courting pursuits, creative approaches, general perception, humor, and the consolidation of self-confidence. The content contained within these volumes can be used also to address many other aspects of business and personal interactions. As a special bonus to the readers, for this first volume, the writers leave the readers with two new and unique proverbial quotes contained within the conclusion.

PART 1

The Ology of Game
The Introduction and
Introspection of Game

Chapter 1 will cover three primary aspects of game. First, we will cover the simple and practical definition of game. Second, we will delve into the aspects of the origin of the word and concept. The last section of this chapter, we'll identify the functional utility of the word and concept and its controversial essence.

Game
The Grammatical Avenue
Manipulating Everything

To begin, from the *Farlex Partner Medical Dictionary* (2012), the definition of ology is "a suffix denoting the study of." The acronym GAME can be understood as the grammatical avenue manipulating everything. This section will combine the ology or the study of game and the acronym GAME, the grammatical avenue manipulating everything, into a streamlined understanding and clarity of the principles. With that, further references in this writing and proceeding volumes will pertain to game as such.

Everyone has heard the saying "He got game" or "She got game." But what is game? In short, the essence of game is simply the ability to *get what you want* in the right situation.

Game's origin acts as a formal guide in transacting with or manipulating the corrupt and informal nature of humanity to get what you want. Like a form of prostitution, from humanity's origins, game has always been. It is the raw ability of one to manipulate another in any manner or fashion. But game does not exist on the boundaries of what we as humanity understand as good and evil. It is instead the aesthetic method of how the message is conveyed and not the message or messenger. Or it is how the point was conveyed and not the point of the message. God has game, and on that same note, so does Satan. They both can achieve their desires and get what they want. This principle applies to politicians, salespeople, and influencers all the same. They have game.

Game is not acquired through or with monetary influence or prevalence. To be as transparent as possible, game cannot be purchased, leased, or borrowed. As an alternative, game is developed. However, monetary gain, influence, prevalence, and a plethora of other things can be achieved with game. That speaks to the manipulative dichotomy of game. More addressing the manipulative and controversial dichotomy of game will be covered in the next section ("Game's Functional Utility").

With that, do you have game? Ask yourself. Then consider, there was a time in your life where either your funds were low, you were not exactly competent, or some semantical thing did not line up with your status. However, if through your mouthpiece, or aka verbal communication, you were still able to gain access or attain the thing you wanted at the time, then, my friend, you have game. Who has game? Anyone with the ability to get what they want in the right situation. So be careful on that note.

That brings us to our first reference to the rules of the game. The rules of the game and that reference for the context of this writing will not refer to an ordinal rule or numbered priority, but instead a rule's functional utility in immediate context of the situation. For context and utility here, the rule of the game is *don't put anything past anyone because anyone is capable of anything.* That rule speaks to the gravity of the situation, and that fact is that you don't know where I come from or what I am capable of, and the same applies to you. Remember to apply all relative rules to all scenarios regularly. The next section will elaborate on the functional use or utility of game as well as elaborate on some of the functional misappropriations of game.

Game's Functional Utility

The functional utility of game refers to an aspect of manipulation. It is in that manipulative area where getting what you want is intertwined with game. And there lies the dichotomy of game. They are intertwined based on the following statement or belief pending your disposition. And why shouldn't you use this powerful tool at your hands to manipulate a better situation or outcome for you and yours? In supplement, the following statement embodies the ultimate controversy of game: *"One will always be manipulated by another."* Unfortunately, that is the inevitable outcome each time. However, game can put you in the position to manipulate the situation as you please. With that, now ask yourself, why not you?

Remember to always introspect into all your situations in life, then question your standings in that situation and press the fact that if you are not manipulating, then you are being manipulated. And on that, another rule of the game: *game recognizes game.* If you can see, hear, or feel it, then so can someone else. Bear in mind this is a belief system in many circles. Another attribute of game is that it provides a metaunderstanding or deeper, intimate understanding of an individual. That in consideration may be why it is easy to recognize.

To address a possible misconception of game, the expression "Drunk with power" or an ability is not a utility of game. It is a blatant exploitation of a precious ability that only aids in the misconception or misinterpretation of game. Those with game should act as and remember that they are representatives of. So it would be prudent to act as a positive representative of game. The previous statements were not declarative by any means, but instead, recall this point of view is better understood as perspectival, influential observations, leaving the reader to glean the content contained within the volumes of the writings as the reader desires.

With that, now consider game as a mental muscle. We know that muscles and muscle groups grow through exercise. So start exercising and or developing game and other critical muscle groups to reach your proper muscle tonus.

The previous statement is a segue into another concept. This concept is loosely understood as *reasonably representing what you wish to achieve or gain.* The word *reasonably* is where the emphasis dwells. Within reason, show others (your presentable package) that which will potentially attract what you seek. Case and point, if you desire that athlete's body style, then you should present your athletic build. Condition your body as such. Why? Because in the best relationships, understanding and reciprocation are the essence of prolific connections, unions, or hookups.

The arrival at yet another rule of the game summarizes this chapter: *put yourself in their shoes and honestly address your own vulnerabilities in that same situation.* Another one of game's many attributes can be described as an intimate metaunderstanding of an individual in a strenuous dilemma. Therefore, an empathetic analyzation when determining an individual's choices in strenuous dilemmas will provide you with a divine ability to properly decipher character.

Chapter Summary / Key Takeaways

Key takeaways from this first chapter include

- identifying the meaning of or definition of game,
- understanding the origin of game, and
- comprehending the functional utility of game and the primary controversy behind it.

The next chapter will address a couple of references or approaches on how to accurately identify and understand character.

CHAPTER 2

Decipher Character

Most people are familiar with *Star Wars* and with the references that pertain to it, so we will begin this chapter with a reference to the main character distinction between the Jedi and the Sith. First, it has been understood that only the Dark Lord of the Sith knows the Sith's and Jedi's weaknesses. But disregard the messenger and consider the message here in context of the principle that is being conveyed. Now the Jedi's weakness is that they are too naive and trusting. For those that can relate to that, adhere to that principle, filter all content, and trust no one.

The following is for those who relate on the other end of that spectrum. Before the Sith Lord Darth Bane, the founder of the rule of two, a law of constraint where only two Sith are permitted at one time, a master and apprentice, the Sith had no order in the hierarchy of Sith Lords (Delatte 2022). That entails the Sith's weakness that they are too self-absorbed and overconfident. In lieu of that, Senator Palpatine was able to manipulate quietly for years, right under the Jedi's noses. He was privy to the dichotomy of the force and was able to easily manipulate what he desired. And he was still able to appease the masses to a certain extent. That type of character is more accurately described by the rap god E-40. The rap god E-40 described this character type as a playertician.

A playertician, for this writing's sake, is the combination of an on-point player and a diabolical politician. So be the playertician in the game. To break the proper character type down further, game's proper muscle tonus lies somewhere between not overestimating yourself or your characteristics and not underestimating others' character and abilities. Another exceptional example based on a similar theme is for those who vibe on the biblical level. Remember, be "wise as serpents and harmless as doves" (Matthew 10:16 KJV). In addition, be creative with your communications and expressions. It only adds to the overall aesthetic appeal of game. More about creativity will be covered in chapter 3. The next section will encourage the reader with the right thought process in any situation.

Know Your Surroundings

This section is paramount. Knowing your surroundings could save your life and the lives of others around you. Social and political unrest is very prevalent, so please be careful in all your pursuits. With the increase in active shooters, the writers have an illustration of a method against active shooters that seems to work efficiently. For example, I am walking into the store or whatever the designated task may be at the time. As I am walking in from the parking lot, I am taking detailed mental notes on the people around me and their apparent moods and demeanor. If anyone or anything appears to be off, I double back and state that I left something in my vehicle. Did I really? No. However, I use that distraction to get a safe distance right behind the person in question. Then carefully and indirectly, I simply observe the person in question until I am satisfied that the person in question is not a threat. If perhaps they turn out to be a threat, then they are completely oblivious to the fact that I have a tactical advantage all over them. This goes back to a direct reference to a rule of the game: *don't put anything past anyone because anyone is capable of anything.*

When carefully observing your surroundings, you will find that action to be very contagious in modern times, and you will not be the only one. Remember, there is great strength in numbers, especially in situations concerning public safety.

Do Not Hesitate

And right off the bat, another rule of the game: *do not hesitate.* Do not hesitate to take any actions (e.g., courtship, advancement in business, self-health, or self-preservation). If the opportunity presents itself, put it in a headlock (please not a literal headlock), but still, run with it. That slight hesitation could be the difference between a good night and a bad night with the acquisition of a new acquaintance or not. Or that slight hesitation could be the difference in someone's life (e.g., a bad character judgment). Regardless of the scenario, absolutely do not hesitate! Who knows if the opportunity will present itself again; either way, no coulda, woulda, shouldas.

Chapter Summary / Key Takeaways

Key takeaways from chapter 2 include the following:

- Be the playertician.
- Know your surroundings.
- *Do not hesitate* (another rule of the game).

The next chapter will cover the creative aspect of game, including an introduction of a familiar and unique character reference and a lighthearted example of humor to help establish a rapport.

PART 2

Angle Your Approach

Within this next section, the reader should start developing their own unique niche on how to effectively angle their approach. Creativity, humor, and uniqueness are all powerful tools at the readers' disposal.

CHAPTER 3

Creativity

In this chapter, we will explore creative communications and expressions with an introduction to characters that bend traditional normative character references. This chapter is also equipped with a quick reference to the funny side of things involving a creative and funny approach.

Be creative with your expressions. For instance, most have heard the expression "You got this" or "I got this." The expression "Got this" alludes to the implication of temporary possession of a task or ability delegated. "Having this," a new and upgraded version of the expression "Got this," alludes to the permanent possession of the function or ability. No longer do we "got this," but instead, now we are "having this" because permanent possession of the facility echoes back to the source. Furthermore, if a task is delegated out, then that ("You got this") means the abilities associated with that task will be reconsolidated back to the source after completion of said task or responsibility. To reiterate, from this point forward, now the expression is we are or that I am "having this" because we exclusively retain the source of the ability to…

Be Unique

As unique goes, stretch your mind with us here, and let's wrap our thoughts on an old ethnic concept rooted in black or African communities across the world. This character type is *the ultimate archetype*. A real nigga ninja. As far as the game is concerned, this character type is the most elite.

Japanese antiquity suggests, "For a Samurai to be brave, he must have a bit of Black blood" (Japanese proverb) (Rashidi 1994). In that context, if that were not the case, then the individual could not identify as a brave samurai. To further intertwine the concepts, samurai warriors and ninjas are known as the most elite (or "glete," the combination of gangsta and elite) warriors across the world. Similarly, the concept of a real nigga, samurai, and ninja are at the pinnacle of their culminations. The phrase real nigga stands on its own true essence. The addition of ninja to real nigga ninja acts as the perfect propitiation to the concept, principle, and expression. To reiterate, this is a belief system in many circles. In retrospect, that also highlights the acknowledgment of black or African influence and their historical contributions across the world. It has come to our attention concerning this very subject that a new Netflix anime series is being produced entitled *The True Story of Yasuke, the Legendary Black Samurai* (Moon 2021). These accounts only further the truth about black- or African-inspired historical events by shining the light on shadowy or misrecorded events in chronicle.

Returning to the matter at hand, for those with the ethnic backgrounds that do not align with the concept of real nigga ninja, *please do not use the phrase or expression* (remember instead to have respect for your surroundings always). As an alternative measure, refer to it as an R. N. ninja. Most folks at that point will fill in the expression with their own ethnic background, screen for everything, then move on and/or complement the substitution or noneffort.

Again, if that specific phrase or expression does not apply to you, then own what does. For instance, I have an Italian friend that swears he is a real Italian ninja. I tell him that that is cute, and from there we agree to disagree; however, I acknowledge his attempt to substitute the reference, and no one was offended in any way, and that is the ultimate point.

For this section, a special type of rapport was developed between the reader and writers. A couple of creative and semicontroversial characters were introduced in this section. The attempt was made to smooth over their introduction with a little comedy. Smooth it over with comedy, or another rule of the game is *be funny*.

Be Funny

This part is intuitive, quick, and simple. There is great utility in humor. Everyone loves the power of a comical person. So please do not underestimate this simple but extremely effective tool at the readers' disposal. Keep in mind that whatever environment you might find yourself in that humor or funny is subjective. So remember, you clowns, be sensitive and witty with all your jokes, and you will not experience many frowns.

Chapter Summary / Key Takeaways

Key takeaways from chapter 3 include the following:

- Use your creativity.
- Be unique.
- *Be funny* (another rule of the game).

The next chapter is designed to inspire an individual with the freedom and wisdom to navigate through and around sensitive situations and topics with the proper application of game. With the contrast and comparison of an illustration, the reader should be able to inspire problem-solving mechanisms to assist them in properly navigating in the game.

CHAPTER 4

Countermechanisms

Follow the comparison and illustration in this short chapter to reach the demonstration and utilization of equilibrium within the concept of countermechanisms.

The following examples are diametrically opposed. They are as far as their fields of study can be apart from one another. However, here we will contrast and compare them. A counterfighter/fighter and a physician. The two are together in harmony in this writing now to exhibit a powerful point of equilibrium.

A Fighter/Counterfighter

A counterfighter does not strike first. Instead, a counterfighter counters the strike of their opponent. Another apt analogy would be like a mental jujitsu. The word *jujitsu* derives from the Japanese words *jū*, meaning "gentle," and *jutsu*, meaning "art" (Culture, Entertainment, Sports 2020). So use the gentle but effective art of game as game jitsu or as a mechanism against anyone in opposition. Do not seek to draw first blood or offend potential acquaintances. Remember to use game as a countermeasure or as a tool to diffuse animosity. Why? Because that's another rule of the game, that's why. *Wise people don't burn bridges; we build them.* There is no profit in the loss of a potential acquaintance or a resource not utilized. That goes back to the old reference of common sense. More about the common sense reference will be covered in chapter 5. To summarize this section, on one hand, be like the counterfighter, always ready to counter a strike gently but effectively, like a form of game jitsu.

Be the Physician

The physician is known by their great knowledge and ability to heal the body. We can derive the physician's modus operandi, a Latin phrase meaning "mode of operating," directly from the Hippocratic Oath (Institute 2020). The Hippocratic Oath states, "First, do no harm" (Shmerling MD, 2020). That is a physician's statement of beliefs, which is fascinating in and of itself. Given that, the Hippocratic Oath's practice correlates clearly for this principle. Do no harm should be a rule of the game. However, it is not; it is common sense. So on the other hand, be like the physician and do no harm.

The brief analogy of the counterfighter and the physician in this chapter acts as an intermediary, supporting both faculties while exhibiting a powerful point of equilibrium. Moreover, the contrast between the counterfighter and physician exemplifies the proper demonstration and utilization of equilibrium within the concept of countermechanisms.

Do not misconstrue; if the shoe fits, wear it. As far as the fighter goes, be the one that is willing and able to stand against negativity and opposition. All adore that courageous character type, so keep that in perspective out there in the game. Furthermore, most individuals would choose to be viewed as creative, courageous, and fearless individuals that stand in the gap. And there are numerous tales in our culture alone that support that account. But keep in mind, the great Sun Tzu, author of *The Art of War*, stated, "The supreme art of war is to subdue the enemy without fighting." To subdue gently and effectively any in opposition of game, that should be the primary goal. The preceding Sun Tzu quote is an apt reiteration and application of the new expression and proper application of game jitsu.

Chapter Summary / Key Takeaways

Chapter 4's key takeaways include the following:

- Be a counterfighter.
- Be like a physician.
- Use game jitsu.

The final chapter will cover the exit principle involved with any interaction, the wrap-up.

CHAPTER 5

The Wrap-Up

This last section is also intuitive, quick, and simple. This concept comes directly from the ingenious comedian Dave Chappelle. On *The Chapelle Show*, Dave Chappelle introduced it as the "Wrap It Up" sketch. The "Wrap It Up" sketch was a hilariously clever sketch involving characters' bad time management in nonproductive situations (Dave Chappelle, Wikipedia, 2022). Beyond coincidence, *"Wrap it up"* is another rule of the game. The last thing most folks want to do is waste time on a nonproductive situation, no matter what it is. In fact, not to chop and screw a rule of the game here, but remember, *put yourself in their shoes,* and let that be a temperature in the room gauge from this point forward.

Common Sense

Unfortunately, most will agree that common sense is no longer common. As a result, use game to feel out dispositions. To delve deeper on that note, the quintessential fact of game is that it is the epitome of both comprehensive and common and is truly an uncanny tool for ambition and understanding. Please keep that in mind when interacting with the diversity of individuals out there in the game. Apply a deciphering perception in your interactions, reasoning, and wisdom, and game will guide you or as the late and great rap god Pimp C stated, "Keep big things popping and li'l things dropping." That precise approach will keep the frivolous matters beneath you and vital matters at your grasp.

Conclusion of volume 1: The content and material covered within this writing was organized to encourage, inform, motivate creativity, inspire self-confidence, and expand potential. Concepts and expressions like "Having this," R. N. ninja, playertician, and the *"Be funny"* rule are exclusively unique to this writing. As stated in the introduction, the writings contained within these volumes are not instructional. They are better understood as perspectival, influential observations. They leave the reader to glean the content contained within the volumes of the writings as the reader desires. Thank you. As a bonus for this first volume, the writers leave the readers with two new and unique proverbial quotes contained within the conclusion.

Chapter Summary / Key Takeaways

Key takeaways from chapter 5 include the following:

- *Wrap it up* (another rule of the game).
- Use common sense.
- Conclusion of volume 1.

Conclusion

The writers sincerely hope that the readers enjoyed this writing just as much as the writers enjoyed writing it. The content of this writing will hopefully open a new avenue of thinking for its readers while streamlining the concepts covered into the ultimate courting approach. From the definition of game in the first chapter to the funny approach in chapter 3 and the "wrap it up" concept in chapter 5, this writing has encompassed a broad and colorful topic range. That specific topic range analyzation, again, can be understood as perspectival, influential observations. With that, the tools are in our hands. Let us use them effectively. Thank you.

The writers leave the readers with two new and unique proverbial quotes that summarizes their collective experiences in the game:

- It is better to be the black sheep in the family rather than another snake in the grass.
- It is better to fight with your back against the wall because then your enemies cannot stab you in the back.

Future volumes of this concept and principle will be available on shelves soon. Please take heed.

Volume 2 will address, in addition to other rules of the game, more unique concepts, principles, expressions, and the evolution of game (demonstrated through the evolved writing style and content). And unlike any other writings of such, we will address theology and the acronym PIMPIN (Put it...).

BIBLIOGRAPHY

Delatte, T. 2022. "Star Wars: 25 Sith from Weakest to Most Powerful, Officially Ranked." The Things. https://www.thethings.com/star-wars-sith-weakest-most-powerful-ranked.

Farlex Partner Medical Dictionary. (2012). Retrieved November 28, 2022, from https://medicaldictionary.thefreedictionary.com/-ology.

Joynson, Travis. 2020 May 20. "Japanese Jiu-Jitsu: History, Evolution, and Success." Culture Exchange. https://culture-exchange.blog/japanese-jiu-jitsu-history-evolution-success/.

Legal Information Institute. 2020 January 7. "Modus Operandi." LII / Legal Information Institute. Law. https://www.law.cornell.edu/wex/modus_operandi.

Moon, K. 2021 April 30. "The True Story of Yasuke, the Legendary Black Samurai Behind Netflix's New Anime Series." Time. https://time.com/6039381/yasuke-black-samurai-truestory/.

Rashidi, R. 2014. "For a Samurai to be brave, he must have a bit of Black blood." Japanese proverb. Rashidi, R. 1994 December 3. "Black Presence Early Japan." Proudblackbuddhist.Org. https://www.proudblackbuddhist.org/Japanese_Are_Racist__A_Lecture/Black_Presence_Early_Japan.html.

ShareAlike License 3.0. 2022 November 28. "Dave Chappelle." Wikipedia. https://en.wikipedia.org/wiki/Dave_Chappelle.

Shmerling, Robert II., MD. 2020 June 22. "First, do no harm." Harvard Health. https://www.health.harvard.edu/blog/first-do-no-harm-201510138421.

Sun Tzu quotes (author of *The Art of War*). https://www.bing.com/search?q=when+was+sun+tzu+art+of+war+written&form=ANNTH1&refig=20d64dc6108a4fc69f3a8ca435eaeb85&sp=6&qs=NM&p

q=when+was+sun+tzu%2C+the+art+of+war+&sk=PRES1N-M5&sc=6-33&cvid=563207c81d3a40e6cac85b545ef73eeb.
The Holy Bible King James Version (KJV) (print). Reference Bible. Matthew 10:16 KJV. 2000. Grand Rapids, Michigan 49530. Published by Zondervan Publishing House.

ABOUT THE AUTHOR

As stated in the introduction, for over two decades of the writers' lives, the ology of game was truly their religion. The ology of game, in correlation with common sense, acts as a true belief system that can produce unnatural results for those who are privy to their benefits. This writing is witness to the fact that game can produce uncanny results for those who utilize it efficiently.

Although as stated previously in this writing, the ology of game was a religion for the writers for many years, nevertheless, things inevitably change. But game does not reduce, fade, or dissipate. Instead, it pivots into things like flourishing marriages, new profitable career avenues, and productive acquaintances and ventures along with beautiful families and legacies that which only exemplify the awesome outcome of game. All those things and many more do the writers of this series enjoy only because the proper application of game in any situation can wield awesome results. The writers are here to tell the readers, regardless of what you don't have, use what you got to get what you want. And thanks again!